Red and Rover

A Boy, a Dog, a Time, a Feeling.

a comic strip by Brian Basset

Andrews McMeel Publishing

Kansas City

Dedicated to the inspiring exploits of:

Alan Shepard
Gus Grissom
John Glenn
Scott Carpenter
Wally Schirra
Deke Slayton
Gordon Cooper

America's Mercury Astronauts

6

7

I DUNNO, RED. OWNING A DOG IS A BIG RESPONSIBILITY.
PLEASE LET ME STAY. PLEASE LET ME STAY.
PLEASE LET ME STAY. PLEASE LET ME STAY.
PLEASE LET ME STAY. PLEASE LET ME STAY.
FINE. HE CAN STAY.
ARF!
BRIAN BASSET
PLEASE LET ME HAVE A RAISE IN MY ALLOWANCE. PLEASE LET ME HAVE A RAISE IN MY ALLOWANCE. PLEASE LET ME HAVE...

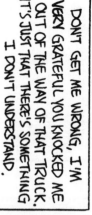

DON'T GET ME WRONG, I'M VERY GRATEFUL YOU KNOCKED ME OUT OF THE WAY OF THAT TRUCK. IT'S JUST THAT THERE'S SOMETHING I DON'T UNDERSTAND.

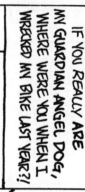

IF YOU REALLY ARE MY GUARDIAN ANGEL DOG, WHERE WERE YOU WHEN I WRECKED MY BIKE LAST YEAR?!

WERE YOU *SERIOUSLY* INJURED??

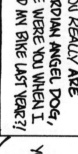

NO, JUST SCRAPED MY HANDS AND KNEES.

THEN I *MUST'VE* BEEN THERE.

BRIAN BASSET

THAT "THING" SPRAWLED OUT ON THE SOFA IS MY BROTHER, MARTIN.

P.U.! SMELLS LIKE <u>DOG</u> IN HERE!

FOLLOW ME.

MOM, MARTIN *HASN'T* SHOWERED IN DAYS.

MARTIN!

BRIAN BASSET

14

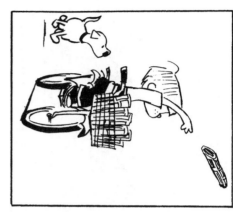

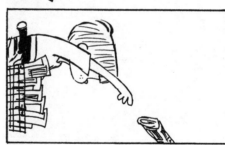

16

HE SURE SEEMED AWFULLY YOUNG TO BE PLAYING "REAL" ARMY THOUGH.

I NEVER KNEW HIM. I'VE ONLY SEEN OLD PHOTOGRAPHS OF HIM.

HE WAS KILLED IN A WAR.

ROVER, WE'LL BE BACK IN A FEW HOURS. WE'RE GOING TO VISIT MY UNCLE JIMMY'S GRAVE.

I MAY HAVE INHERITED MY MOTHER'S SUNNY DISPOSITION, BUT I GOT MY FATHER'S *SAD* PUPPY EYES!

GO AWAY! SCRAM! I'M *NOT* TAKING YOU FOR A WALK RIGHT NOW.

BRIAN BASSET

SOMETIMES I'M TORN BETWEEN FINDING A JOB OR STAYING HOME WITH THE BOYS.

CAROL, WE'VE DISCUSSED THIS MANY TIMES.

BRIAN BASSET

...IT'S PROBABLY BEST FOR YOUR SANITY THAT YOU WORK.

I LOVE TV DINNERS!

DO YOU LOVE THE LITTLE SQUARE OF MASHED POTATO PART, OR THE LITTLE SQUARE OF PEACH COBBLER PART?

I LOVE THE TV PART.

BRIAN BASSET

20

TEST 'EM OUT! SEE IF YOUR **NEW TENNIES** REALLY DO LET YOU "JUMP HIGHER."

BRIAN BASSET

PERSONALLY, I THINK YOU CAN JUMP HIGHER WHEN YOU'RE **NOT** WEIGHED DOWN BY SHOES.

ONCE AND FOR ALL, LET'S SEE IF THESE NEW TENNIES REALLY **ARE FASTER** THAN MY OLD ONES.

SAY "WHEN."

WOOF!

BRIAN BASSET

WELL?! ARE THEY FASTER?!

I'LL SAY! YOUR OLD PAIR BARELY MOVED.

23

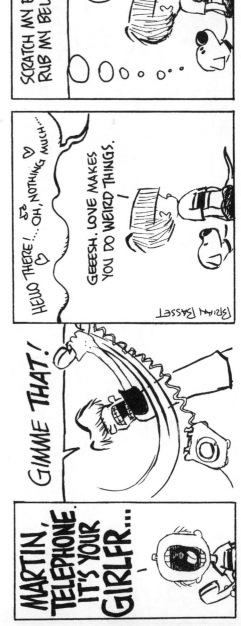

24

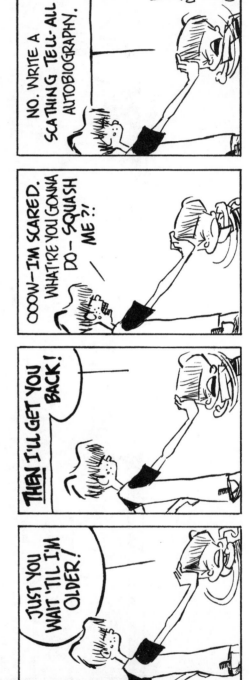

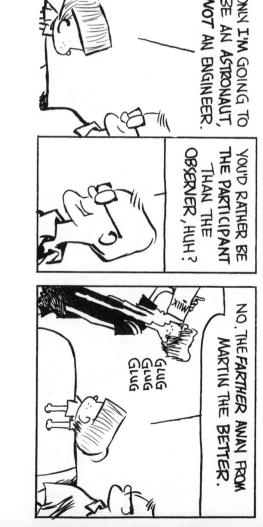

Y'KNOW, IT WOULDN'T KILL YOU TO ADMIT YOU CAN'T FIND THE STICK I THREW.
I HAVEN'T THE SLIGHTEST IDEA WHAT YOU'RE TALKING ABOUT.
BRIAN BASSET

SWEETHEART, HAVE YOU SEEN RED?

I BELIEVE HE AND ROVER ARE IN THE GARAGE WORKING ON SOME KIND OF LUNAR ORBITER.

BRIAN BASSET

HEH-HEH. THAT BOY'S INTEREST IN SPACE EXPLORATION HAS REALLY BLASTED OFF SINCE I GAVE HIM THAT TELESCOPE.

"...AND ON THE MOON I WON'T HAVE TO GO TO SCHOOL!"

BRIAN BASSET

HEY! MY DAD'S AN AEROSPACE ENGINEER—Y'KNOW, A ROCKET SCIENTIST. MAYBE HE CAN HELP US WITH OUR SPACE CAPSULE AND LUNAR LANDER.

IT NEVER HURTS TO ASK.

DAD, D'YA THINK YOU COULD BRING ME HOME SOMETHING LIKE THE INTERNAL GUIDANCE SYSTEM TO A SATURN Ⅴ ROCKET?

SURE. RIGHT AFTER I BRING YOU HOME SOME KEROSENE, LIQUID HYDROGEN, AND LIQUID OXYGEN.

WE'RE IN LUCK!

ARF!

MOM. GUS WANTS TO KNOW IF I CAN CAMP OUT IN HIS BACKYARD TONIGHT?

SHE SAID "YES"

(AHEM) YOUR SLEEPING BAG'S WAGGING.

LATER...

GO AWAY! I CAN'T BELIEVE YOU "KISSED" ANOTHER KID!

HE HAD S'MORES ALL OVER HIS FACE.

LICK

I WISH I HAD A DOG LIKE ROVER. HE'S THE BEST!

I'M SO GLAD ROVER COULD CAMP OUT WITH US!

ME TOO!

BRIAN BASSET

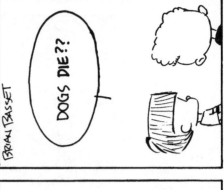

35

HERE'S THE PITCH...
BELTED! DEEP TO CENTER FIELD! WAYYYY BACK!...
THAT BALL IS..... OUT'TA HERE! IT'S A HOMERUN!
UM... EVER CONSIDERED A CAREER IN BROADCASTING?
BRIAN BASSET

39

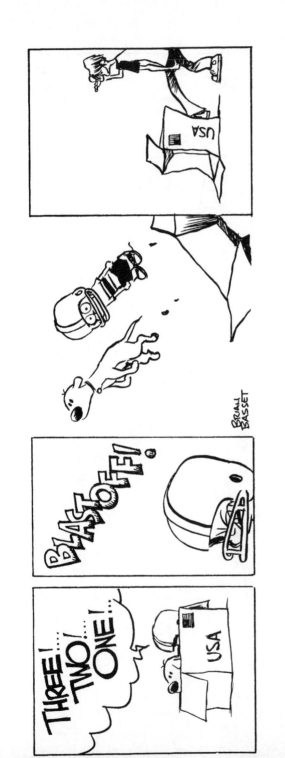

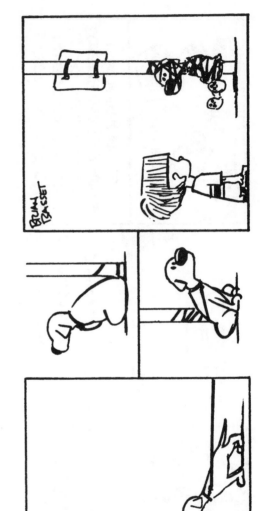

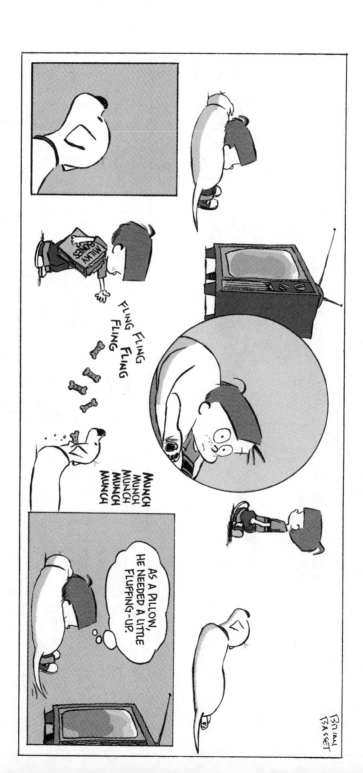

ALL I DID WAS GIVE HIM A "LASSIE" EPISODE UPDATE.

NO THANKS. I HAVE PLENTY.

COME ON! WE'VE GOTTA GET HELP!!

BRIAN BASSET

ARF ARF ARF ARF ARF ARF ARF

TIMMY'S FALLEN DOWN A WELL OUT BEHIND THE OLD JOHNSON PLACE?!?

WHAT IS IT, BOY?!

FLEAS?

SCRATCH SCRATCH SCRATCH SCRATCH SCRATCH SCRATCH SCRATCH SCRATCH SCRATCH SCRATCH SCRATCH SCRATCH

SCRATCH SCRATCH

BRIAN BASSET

AND THE SUICIDE SQUEEZE PLAY CATCHES *EVERYONE* COMPLETELY OFF GUARD!

I JUST STRUCK OUT A *GREAT* BATTER!

BIP!

RUNNER ON THIRD ....TWO DOWN.... HERE'S THE PITCH!...

BRIAN BASSET

TWO ON, TWO OUT, TWO STRIKES, BOTTOM OF THE NINTH--- HERE'S THE PITCH!...

BRIAN BASSET

48

IT'S A P-51 MUSTANG THAT JUST CRASH LANDED AFTER THE PILOT BAILED OUT!

EVER HEAR OF DIRECTIONS?!

BRIAN BASSET

WHAT IS THAT ??!

A P-51 MUSTANG.

The War Department regrets to inform you that....

TELEPHONE! I GOT IT!

RING

BUMP!

HERE'S THE B-17 FLYING FORTRESS ON A DARING DAYLIGHT BOMBING RAID DEEP INTO HOSTILE ENEMY TERRITORY.

BRIAN BASSET

I'M TIRED OF MARTIN PUSHING ME AROUND! WHAT I NEED ARE MUSCLES!

BRIAN BASSET

CHARLES ATLAS SAYS HE CAN TRANSFORM ME FROM A 90-POUND WEAKLING TO **THIS** IN JUST SIX SHORT WEEKS!

TROUBLE IS...

I'VE GOTTA GET TO 90 POUNDS FIRST.

I'LL HELP YOU TRAIN!

MILK

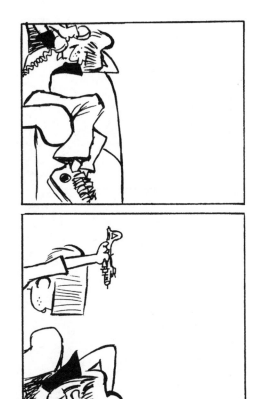

UM, HANG ON A SEC. I'M ABOUT TO BE BOMBED.

DANG. HIS AIR-DEFENSE SYSTEM IS MORE SOPHISTICATED THAN I THOUGHT.

BRIAN BASSET

54

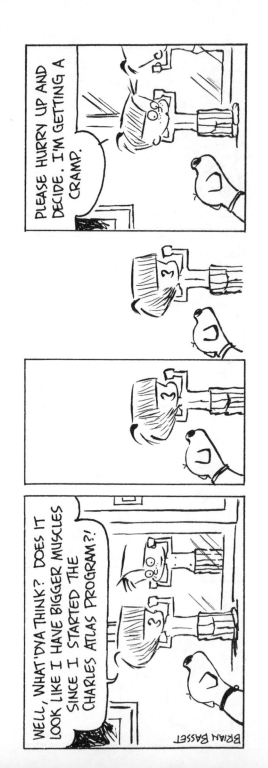

TEN!... NINE!...
NASA
EIGHT!...SEVEN
NASA
...SIX!...FIVE!...
ER, COMMANDER.
NASA
...FOUR!...
THREE!... TWO!....
WON'T CARDBOARD BURN UP RATHER EASILY DURING RE-ENTRY?
NASA
THIS IS PRECISELY WHY CHRISTOPHER COLUMBUS DIDN'T HAVE A DOG AS HIS FIRST MATE.
BRIAN BASSET

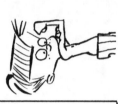

AUNT HELEN SENT ME AN INSTAMATIC CAMERA FOR MY BIRTHDAY, AND I WANT YOU TO BE MY FIRST SUBJECT, ROVER!

SNAP SNAP SNAP SNAP SNAP SNAP SNAP

SNAP SNAP SNAP SNAP SNAP SNAP SNAP SNAP SNAP

BRIAN BASSET

Dear Aunt Helen:
Thank you for the swell camera.
You forgot money for film developing though.

YEAH, BABY, YEAH! THAT'S IT, BABY! YEAH!

SNAP SNAP SNAP SNAP

OH, BABY, YEAH. LIKE THAT, BABY! YEAH, BABY, YEAH, BABY!!

SNAP SNAP SNAP SNAP

BRIAN BASSET

YEAH, PUPPY, YEAH! OH, PUPPY, YEAH! THAT'S IT, PUPPY! YEAH, PUPPY!

SNAP SNAP SNAP SNAP

P.S.
If you don't use him we'll switch brands.

Dear Barko dog Food Co.
As a lifelong, loyal customer, I think my dog, Rover, should have his picture on every can of your fabulous dog food.

I've included a recent photo of him so you can see just how handsome he is.

BRIAN BASSET

Actually I have. And it could use a bit less salt.

In fact, he's so handsome, his photo should be on every can of your fine dog food. I know it would make me want to eat it!

BRIAN BASSET

Dear Barko DogFood Co.
My Dog, Rover, is the most handsome dog in the whole world.

SORRY. I JUST DON'T SEE WHAT ALL THE FUSS IS OVER "BELLY RUBS"

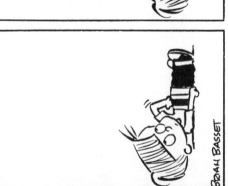

BRIAN BASSET

I PUT YOUR PHOTO IN AN ENVELOPE... YOU LICKED THE STAMP.... WE PUT THE ENVELOPE IN THE MAILBOX....

BRIAN BASSET

I CAN'T FIGURE OUT WHY WE HAVEN'T HEARD BACK FROM THE BARKO DOG FOOD COMPANY BY NOW?

SIGH.

HERE, LET ME TAKE YOUR SHOES OFF FOR YOU, DAD. I'M SURE YOU'VE HAD A TOUGH DAY.

I'LL BE RIGHT BACK WITH YOUR SLIPPERS.

BRIAN BASSET

WHAT'DYA MEAN YOU CHEWED UP HIS SLIPPERS?!?

SLIPPERS ARE SO RUDDY-DUDDY, DAD. HOW 'BOUT AN ULTRA COOL PAIR OF FLIP-FLOPS?!!

ARF! ARF!

ARF! ARF! ARF! ARF! ARF!

FINE. I'LL DEFEND YOU AGAINST ALL CHARGES OF CHEWING UP DAD'S SLIPPERS ON **ONE** CONDITION.

...YOU TAKE THE LEATHER OUT OF YOUR MOUTH BEFORE WE GO TO TRIAL.

BRIAN BASSET

WELL??

I'D SUGGEST YOU HIRE A NEW ATTORNEY, BUT I COULD REALLY USE THE MONEY FOR CANDY.

RATHER, HIS **REAL** INTENTION WAS TO CHEW UP YOUR SHOES, *NOT* YOUR SLIPPERS.

DAD. I KNOW IT DOESN'T LOOK GOOD FOR MY CLIENT, BUT YOU'VE GOTTA BELIEVE HIM—HE *NEVER* INTENDED TO CHEW UP YOUR SLIPPERS.

BRIAN BASSET

WELL??

WITH GOOD BEHAVIOR, I THINK I CAN HAVE YOU OUT IN 340 DOG YEARS.

I THINK NOT. AFTER ALL, YOU SAW THE SIZE OF THE BITE MARKS HE LEFT IN THE LEATHER.

DO YOU HONESTLY THINK THEY'D BE FOOLISH ENOUGH TO TESTIFY AGAINST MY CLIENT?!

BRIAN BASSET

THERE ARE NO WITNESSES. AND IF THERE WERE...

YOUR HONOR. HOW CAN WE BE ABSOLUTELY CERTAIN IT WAS ROVER WHO ATE YOUR SLIPPERS?

68

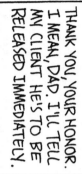

THANK YOU, YOUR HONOR. I MEAN, DAD. I'LL TELL MY CLIENT HE'S TO BE RELEASED IMMEDIATELY.

BRIAN BASSET

THROW THE BOOK AT HIM.

YOU WERE SNOOPING AROUND IN MY ROOM AGAIN, WEREN'T YOU?!!

NO, I WAS LOOKING FOR ROVER!

WHAT WAS YOUR DOG DOING IN MY ROOM??

BRIAN BASSET

PROBABLY GASPING FOR AIR.

IN THE MORNING I START A NEW SCHOOL YEAR AND YOU CAN'T COME WITH ME, BOY. SORRY.

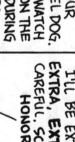
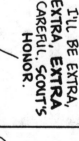

BUT **I'M** YOUR GUARDIAN ANGEL DOG. WHO'S GONNA WATCH OUT FOR YOU ON THE MONKEY BARS DURING RECESS??

BRIAN BASSET

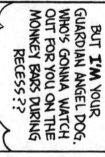

I'LL BE EXTRA, **EXTRA**, **EXTRA** CAREFUL. SCOUT'S HONOR.

IT'S FOR MY DOG. DON'T ASK.

HAVE A GREAT FIRST DAY BACK AT SCHOOL, SWEETIE.

KISS

MOMMMMM

BRIAN BASSET

SLOBBER SLOBBER SLOBBER SLOBBER SLOBBER SLOBBER

71

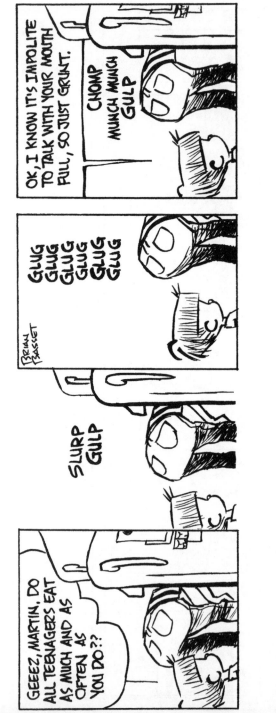

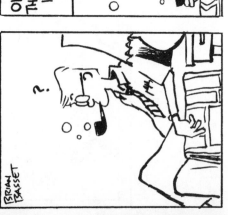

RED, TIME TO GET UP FOR SCHOOL.

WE'RE NOT COMING OUT TILL DAD QUITS SMOKING!

RED, YOU'VE MADE YOUR POINT. YOUR FATHER'S TAKING YOUR CONCERN INTO CONSIDERATION.

NOT GOOD ENOUGH!

YOU HEARD YOUR MOM. YOUR DAD'S TAKING IT INTO CONSIDERATION.

SAYY— WHOSE SIDE ARE YOU ON ANYWAY?!?

THE SIDE THAT LETS ME OUTSIDE FIRST!!

UM, YOU DON'T KNOW WHEN YOU MIGHT BE FIXING LIVER OR BRUSSELS SPROUTS AGAIN, DO YOU?

WHATEVER IT TAKES TO RAISE PUBLIC AWARENESS!

NEXT, I'M THINKING OF GOING ON A HUNGER STRIKE!

I'M STILL GOING TO PROTEST DAD'S SMOKING. I ONLY CAME OUT OF MY ROOM AND ENDED MY "SIT-IN" 'CAUSE OF ROVER.

BRIAN BASSET

LITTLE BROTHER, ME AND THE GUYS ARE PLAYING FOOTBALL NEXT DOOR AND WE COULD REALLY USE YOU.

ME?? YOU WANT ME?!

FOR A CLASS ASSIGNMENT WE HAD TO TRACE OUR FAMILY ANCESTRY, AND GUESS WHAT— I HAVE POLISH, IRISH, AND GERMAN IN ME.

I HAVE GERMAN IN ME TOO!

SHEPHERD?

BRIAN BASSET

WHAT POSITION ARE YOU AGAIN?

THE CORNER OF THE ENDZONE.

BRATWURST.

BRIAN BASSET

SOMETIMES I WONDER IF EARTH WILL EVER BE INVADED BY CREATURES FROM ANOTHER GALAXY.

SOME TIME BEFORE NEXT WEDNESDAY WOULD BE NICE. ...I HAVE A MATH TEST THAT DAY.

BRIAN BASSET

OKAY, *NOW* WHAT AM I THINKING?

BRIAN BASSET

MOM SAYS YOU AND I ARE SO CLOSE WE CAN READ EACH OTHER'S THOUGHTS.

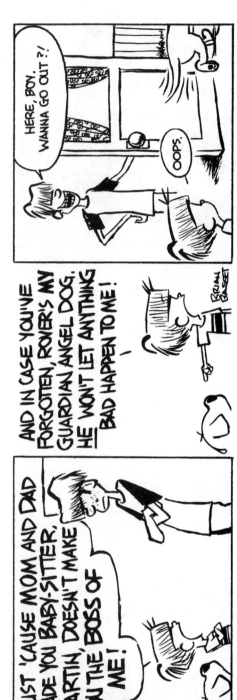

AND THIS IS MY HUSBAND CHARLIE.

YOUR LOVELY WIFE TELLS US YOU WORK FOR THE SPACE PROGRAM.

HEH-HEH, A REAL ROCKET SCIENTIST.

BRIAN BASSET

ACTUALLY, I'M A DROID.

OK, OK, BUT AMONG FELLOW AEROSPACE ENGINEERS, THAT JOKE IS CONSIDERED QUITE FUNNY.

OOPS, I DROPPED A FRENCH FRY.

FIVE-SECOND RULE! IF YOU PICK IT UP WITHIN FIVE SECONDS IT'S **STILL** GOOD.

DOGS BELIEVE IN THE **FIVE-WEEK** RULE.

BRIAN BASSET

MOM MUST REALLY THINK I'M SICK AND NOT JUST FAKING IT.

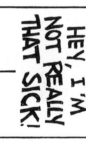

BRIAN BASSET

SHE EVEN TOOK ROVER OUT OF MY ROOM SO HE DOESN'T CATCH WHATEVER I.....

HEY, I'M NOT REALLY THAT SICK!

OOPS.

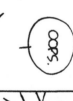

DID YOU SAY SOMETHING, DEAR?

UM...YES, WHEN CAN I HAVE VISITORS?

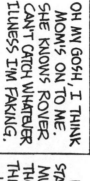

OH MY GOSH, I THINK MOM'S ON TO ME. SHE KNOWS ROVER CAN'T CATCH WHATEVER ILLNESS I'M FAKING.

BRIAN BASSET

LETTING ME STAY HOME "SICK" MUST BE ONE OF THOSE "LESSON" THINGS PARENTS LIKE TO DO.

IT'S ROVER I FEEL BAD FOR. HE WAS REALLY LOOKING FORWARD TO SPENDING THE WHOLE DAY WITH ME.

POOR GUY. HE MUST BE JUST MISERABLE.

SCRATCH SCRATCH SCRATCH

87

88

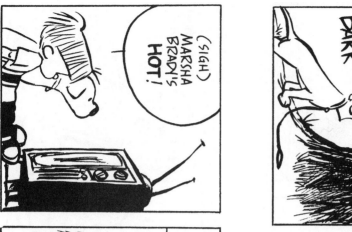

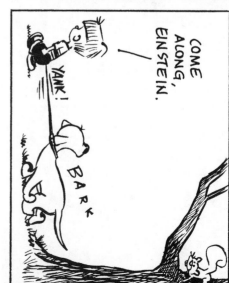

Dear Marsha Brady,

I think you're a fox!

My dog Rover, however, thinks your long hair makes you look like an Afghan hound.

I'M THINKING OF OPENING A LEMONADE STAND.

I KNOW, I KNOW, **WHO** IN THEIR RIGHT MIND DRINKS LEMONADE **THIS** TIME OF YEAR, RIGHT?!

LEMONADE ADDICTS!

PEOPLE PAY MORE WHEN THINGS ARE HARD TO GET.

BRIAN BASSET

HASN'T ANYONE TOLD YOU IT'S NO LONGER LEMONADE SEASON?!

BRIAN BASSET

BRRR. THERE'S A REAL CHILL IN THE AIR. MAYBE OPENING A LEMONADE STAND **THIS** TIME OF YEAR WASN'T SO SMART.

I'LL BE FIRST IN COMMAND, YOU'LL BE SECOND IN COMMAND.

SHOULD ANYTHING HAPPEN TO ME IN THE HEAT OF BATTLE YOU'RE TO TAKE OVER. ANY QUESTIONS?

WHY ARE WE AT WAR?

BRIAN BASSET

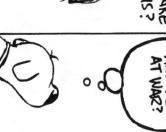

ARE YOU QUESTIONING A SUPERIOR OFFICER?!

THE GARAGE WILL BE AN ENEMY PILLBOX, AND THE CHEVY IN THE DRIVEWAY A PANZER TANK.

OUR OBJECTIVE IS TO SEIZE BOTH THROUGH WHATEVER MEANS POSSIBLE.

PERSONALLY, I VOTE FOR FORECLOSURE AND REPOSSESSION.

BRIAN BASSET

THAT'S THE MADSON'S HOUSE. THEY GIVE OUT HOMEMADE POPCORN BALLS WRAPPED IN COLORED CELLOPHANE.
A MUST STOP!
NEXT DOOR TO THEM ARE THE PUTZEL'S. MRS. PUTZEL MAKES CARAMEL APPLES TO DIE FOR!
WE SHOULD DROP BY THERE EARLY BEFORE THEY RUN OUT.
ACROSS THE STREET LIVES DR. HOLLEY, THE DENTIST. HE USED TO GIVE OUT CHOCOLATE BARS AND SUCKERS.
(SIGH) NOW HE HANDS OUT TOOTHBRUSHES AND A LECTURE.
BRIAN BASSET
NO NEED TO LOSE PRECIOUS TIME THERE.
SCRATCH SCRATCH
REMEMBER, THE MORE YOU PUT INTO TRICK OR TREATING... THE MORE YOU PUT INTO YOUR TUMMY.

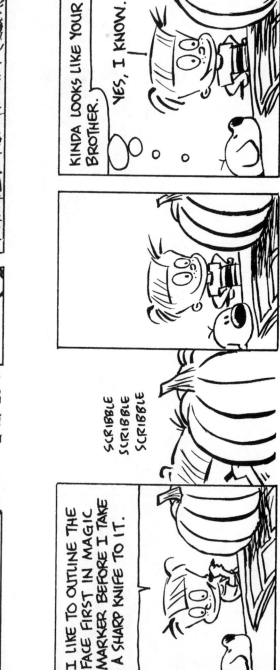

DING DONG

TRICK OR TREAT!

TRICK!...

AWWW, WHAT AN ADORABLE DOGGY.

BRIAN BASSET

BRIAN BASSET

TRICK OR TREAT!

...OR TREAT.

97

66

STAN.

BRIAN BASSET

DO YOU REALLY THINK WE'LL GO INTO SPACE TOGETHER SOME DAY?

ABSOLUTELY! WHERE **I** GO, _YOU_ GO!

HUSTLE, RED. THE BUS WILL BE HERE SOON.

OK, OK, I LOVE YOU, TOO!

THEY'RE SALTY WHEN THEY'RE NERVOUS.

KISS KISS SLOBBER SLOBBER KISS KISS

I HAVE THIS **HUGE** MATH TEST TOMORROW THAT I KNOW I'M GOING TO FLUNK. I'M **HORRIBLE** AT MATH. IN FACT, I'M HORRIBLE AT JUST ABOUT **EVERYTHING.**

Brian Basset

BRIAN BASSET

ARF ARF ARF

CLICK

IT'S THE MIDDLE OF THE NIGHT—WHAT IS IT BOY?

I HEARD A NOISE. LET'S GO DOWNSTAIRS TO INVESTIGATE.

OK, WE'RE DOWNSTAIRS. WHAT DID YOU HEAR?

MY TUMMY. I'M HUNGRY.

WOW. YOUR TUMMY REALLY IS GROWLING.

BUT IT'S NEARLY THREE O'CLOCK IN THE MORNING! IF I GIVE YOU SOMETHING TO EAT NOW, WON'T IT SPOIL YOUR APPETITE FOR BREAKFAST?

BRIAN BASSET

IS THIS A TRICK QUESTION?

LUCKY DOG.

RED, I DON'T WANT YOU SITTING SO CLOSE TO THE TV—IT'S NOT GOOD FOR YOUR EYES!

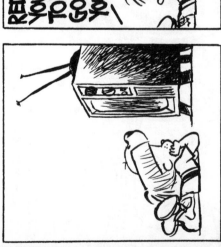

I WAS. YOU WERE THE ONE FEEDING ME!

OH. FOR A MOMENT I THOUGHT YOU WERE DREAMING ABOUT ME.

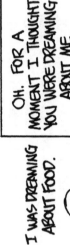

I WAS DREAMING ABOUT FOOD.

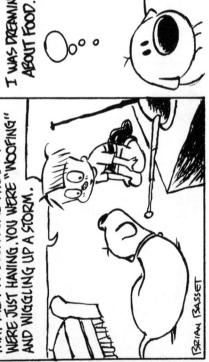

THAT MUST'VE BEEN SOME DREAM YOU WERE JUST HAVING. YOU WERE "WOOFING" AND WIGGLING UP A STORM.

102

SORRY, ROVER. DAD SAID YOU CAN'T COME BOWLING WITH US.

BUT WHO'S GOING TO RETRIEVE YOUR BALL FOR YOU??

DAD SAID THE AUTOMATED BALL RETURN MACHINE WILL DO IT.

BESIDES, REMEMBER WHAT HAPPENED WHEN WE PRACTICED OUT IN THE BACKYARD?

UH-HUH.

DAD, I TOLD THE GUY BEHIND THE RENTAL SHOE COUNTER YOU'D LEAVE HIM A *REALLY* BIG TIP.

...*NEVER* BEEN TOUCHED BY A SWEATY, SMELLY HUMAN FOOT IN THEIR LIFE.

YOU'RE RIGHT! LEMME GRAB YOU A PAIR OF OUR SPECIAL "MECHANICALLY" BROKEN-IN BOWLING SHOES!

HERE YA' GO, KID, SIZE FIVE!

WAIT. THOSE LOOK LIKE THEY'VE BEEN WORN BY OTHER PEOPLE BEFORE.

BRIAN BASSET

104

PACK 57, I'M YOUR NEW DEN MOTHER, MRS. STEVENS, TOMMY'S MOM. ANY — QUESTIONS?

WHEN DO WE GET POCKET KNIVES?!

DO WE EVER GET TO MAKE FIRES??

HOW 'BOUT ARCHERY?

REFRESH MY MEMORY. WHY DID YOUR LAST DEN MOTHER QUIT?

SHE HAD TROUBLE WITH KNOTS.

SHE COULDN'T UNTIE THEM.

YES, RED, WHAT IS IT?

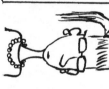

INSTEAD OF A SING-ALONG, CAN WE PLACE A CAN OF BAKED BEANS IN THE FIRE AND WATCH IT EXPLODE?

I HARDLY THINK MY NEIGHBORS WOULD APPRECIATE A CAMP FIRE AT THIS HOUR.

NO, IN YOUR FIREPLACE.

BRIAN BASSET

105

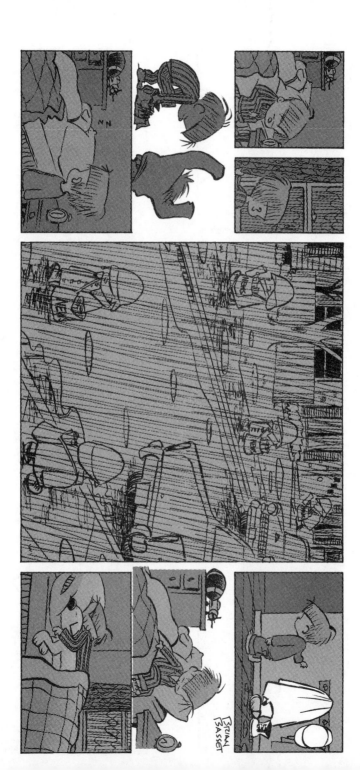

107

MY TEACHER GOT KINDA ANNOYED WITH ME TODAY.

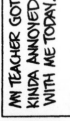

AFTER RECESS WE WERE ALL SUPPOSED TO MAKE PILGRIMS AND TURKEYS OUT OF CONSTRUCTION PAPER AND PASTE.

ONLY, I GAVE MY TURKEY SUPER HERO-LIKE POWERS SO HE CAN MELT GUN BARRELS AND AXE BLADES!

I FIGURE IT'S TIME THE TURKEYS CAME OUT ON TOP!

DOES THIS MEAN NO GIBLETS AND GIZZARDS IN MY BOWL??

BRIAN BASSET

MOM, IS THE TURKEY READY?

IT IS! PLEASE SEND YOUR FATHER IN HERE TO CARVE IT.

OOH, THIS COULD GET INTERESTING.

WHAT'S THE SCORE OF THE GAME DAD?

ALL TIED UP WITH TWO MINUTES LEFT IN REGULATION.

BRIAN BASSET

LET ME TELL YOU A LITTLE ABOUT TONIGHT'S SPECIAL.

THEN HEAPED ALL TOGETHER AND TOPPED WITH A SAVORY CONGEALED BROWN SAUCE.

WE HAVE A NICE DOMESTIC FOWL, CHILLED AND CUT INTO SMALL BITE-SIZED PIECES!...

...COMBINED WITH TWICE-HEATED GREEN BEANS, "POTATOES À LA THURSDAY," AND AN AGED BREAD STUFFING TO DIE FOR!...

flip

MORE RESTAURANTS WOULD BE *SUCCESSFUL* IF THEY SERVED LEFTOVERS *CREATIVELY* AND WELCOMED *DOGS* AS *CUSTOMERS*.

IT'S TRUE! WE ALMOST *NEVER* COMPLAIN AND WE CLEAN OUR OWN DISHES!

UM, WOULD SOMEONE PLEASE GO AFTER RED AND REMIND HIM THAT THAT WAS ONLY THE SECOND-PERIOD BELL.

BRIAN BASSET

RINNNNG

LICK LICK LICK LICK LICK LICK LICK LICK LICK LICK LICK LICK LICK LICK LICK LICK LICK LICK LICK LICK LICK LICK

Z

Z

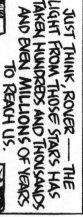

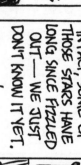

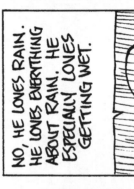

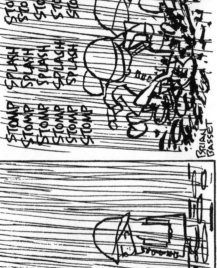

OH MY GOSH !... THE INFAMOUS SQUIRREL-CHASING INCIDENT !

THEY SAY SANTA KNOWS IF YOU'VE BE NAUGHTY OR NICE.

BRIAN BASSET

Dear Santa,
As Rover's Attorney, I want to make it clear that my client was not the one being bad. The Squirrel he chased provoked him!

AND HE WAS THREE HOUSES AWAY FROM COMING INTO OUR YARD TOO!

114

THIS ONE'S CLEAN.

BRIAN BASSET

I'M CHECKING ALL MY PAST CHRISTMAS GIFTS.

FOR DEFECTS?

NO, FOR TINY SURVEILLANCE EQUIPMENT. I'VE GOTTA FIGURE OUT HOW SANTA KNOWS WHEN I'VE BEEN NAUGHTY AND WHEN I'VE BEEN NICE.

YOU'RE RIGHT, SANTA WOULD NEVER SPY ON ME.

MORE LIKELY, THERE'S A "MOLE" IN OUR FAMILY PROVIDING FALSE INFORMATION DIRECTLY TO THE NORTH POLE.

BUT WHO?

BRIAN BASSET

BRIAN BASSET

DOES SHE MEAN FOR US TO EAT IT, OR LINE THE INSIDE OF OUR COATS WITH IT?

IT'S EXTREMELY COLD OUT THIS MORNING SO I MADE YOU BOTH A NICE, PIPING HOT BOWL OF OATMEAL.

BRIAN BASSET

IF YOU ASK ME, PRISON REHABILITATION IS *NOT* WORKING ON THAT BOY.

ONLY TO STEAL IT AGAIN THE FOLLOWING YEAR.

EVERY YEAR THE GRINCH STEALS CHRISTMAS, AND EVERY YEAR HE RETURNS IT.

BRIAN BASSET

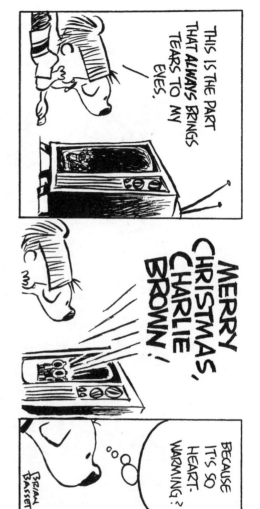

Dear Santa.
Just in case one of your reindeer pulls up lame, my dog Rover makes a terrific reindeer! See enclosed photos.
I CAN'T PROMISE I'LL BE ABLE TO GET YOU FIRST DIBS ON THE BEST TOYS.
SNAP
SNAP
SNAP
SNAP
SNAP
SNAP SNAP
SNAP SNAP
SNAP
SNAP SNAP
SNAP
SNAP
SNAP
SNAP
BRIAN BASSET

FIRST OF ALL, SANTA, I'D REALLY LIKE TO APOLOGIZE FOR THE WAY I ACTED SIX YEARS AGO.

?

REMEMBER HOW I KICKED AND SCREAMED AND KNEED YOU IN THE HEAD WHEN MY PARENTS TRIED TO PUT ME ON YOUR LAP?

NO, BUT IF YOU SAY SO.

WHOA! I MUST'VE KNOCKED HIM IN THE NOGGIN HARDER THAN I THOUGHT.

BRIAN BASSET

SANTA, MY CHRISTMAS LIST.

A "DATE WITH MARCIA BRADY?"

AREN'T YOU A BIT YOUNG?

AREN'T YOU A BIT OLD TO BE WEARING PAJAMAS OUT IN PUBLIC?

BRIAN BASSET

121

ONE "JUNIOR-ASTRONAUT MISSION COMMANDER SPACE HELMET, SIZE MEDIUM."

I PLAN ON GOING INTO SPACE SOMEDAY.

ONE "JUNIOR-ASTRONAUT MISSION COMMANDER SPACE HELMET, SIZE LARGE."

IT'S FOR MY DOG, ROVER. HE PLANS ON COMING WITH ME AND HE'S GOT A BIG SNOUT.

SOUNDS AS IF YOU'VE BEEN EXTRA GOOD THIS YEAR, RED. ADOPTING A HOMELESS DOG IS A FINE THING TO DO!

YOU'RE A DOG LOVER?

SANTA'S AN ANIMAL LOVER OF ALL TYPES.

IF IT HELPS, I ONCE WANTED TO BRING AN ELEPHANT HOME FROM THE CIRCUS BUT MY PARENTS WOULDN'T LET ME.

122

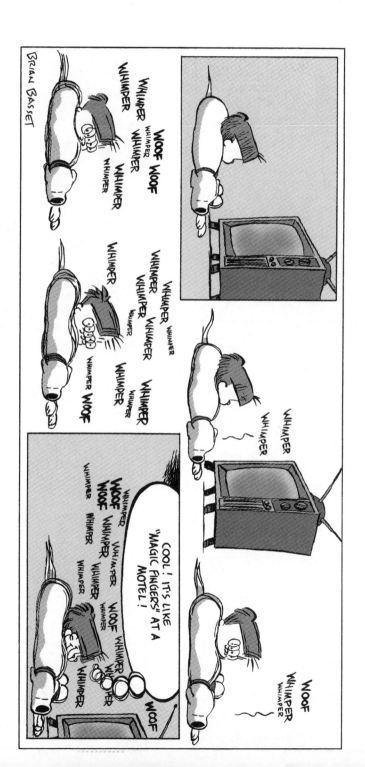

I CAN'T BELIEVE SANTA BROUGHT ME THE SPACE HELMET I WANTED!

NOW I CAN GO TO THE DEEPEST REACHES OF SPACE!... JUST LIKE A REAL ASTRONAUT

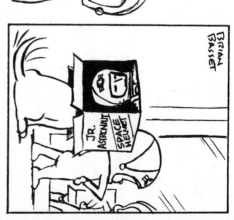

BRIAN BASSET

RED, WE DON'T WEAR SPACE HELMETS AT THE DINNER TABLE.

BRIAN BASSET

WHAT'RE WE HAVING?

CREAM OF LEFTOVERS AND BRUSSELS SPROUTS.

OH YES WE DO.

FLIP

126

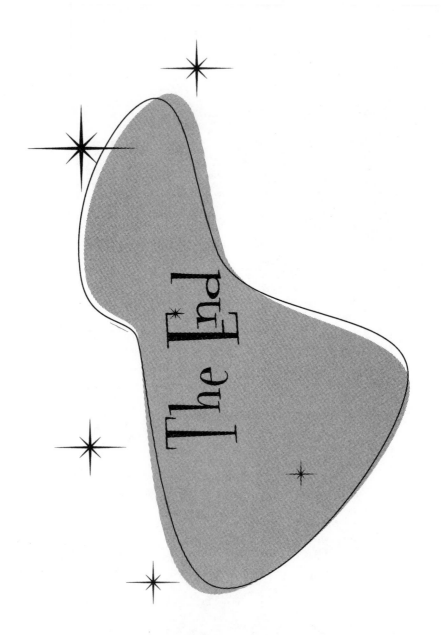